W9-AAE-323

Kylie Jean

Rodeo Craft Queen

by Mary Meinking and Marci Peschke
illustrated by Tuesday Mourning

PICTURE WINDOW BOOKS
a capstone imprint

Editor: Shelly Lyons
Designer: Tracy Davies McCabe
Craft Project Creator: Marcy Morin
Photo Stylist: Sarah Schuette
Art Director: Nathan Gassman
Production Specialist: Laura Manthe

Picture Window Books are published by Capstone
1710 Roe Crest Drive,
North Mankato, Minnesota 56003
www.capstonepub.com

Library of Congress Cataloging-in-Publication Data
Meinking, Mary and Marci Peschke.
Kylie Jean rodeo craft queen /
by Mary Meinking and Marci Peschke.
pages cm — (Nonfiction picture books. Kylie Jean
craft queen.)
Audience: Age 7-9. Audience: Grades K to 3.
Summary: "Introduces crafts related to the book Kylie
Jean rodeo queen, by Marci Peschke"— Provided
by publisher.
Includes bibliographical references and index.
ISBN 978-1-4795-2190-6 (library binding)
1. Handicraft—Juvenile literature. 2. Rodeos—
Juvenile literature. 3. Rodeos in art—Juvenile
literature. I. Peschke, M. (Marci). Rodeo queen. II.
Title. III. Title: Rodeo craft queen.
TT160.M4234 2014
745.5—dc23   2013032215

Photo Credits
All photos by Capstone Studio/Karon Dubke
Design elements: Shutterstock

Printed in the United States of America in Brainerd, Minnesota.
092013   007770BANGS14

Table of Contents

Howdy y'all! It's me, Kylie Jean. You're going to love this book of fantastic rodeo crafts. If you can cut, glue, staple, and paint, then you can make my craft projects. They're so easy, anyone can do them ... well, maybe not my dog, Ugly Brother, but he can help. He likes glitter and glue. I do too!

Do you want to learn how to make your very own cowgirl outfit? You'll have it all: the Rodeo Queen hat, belt buckle, lucky purse, and cowgirl vest. Now giddyap and get your supplies together. You're going to have more fun than a cowgirl with her horse!

TOOLS NEEDED

- acrylic paint
- fabric scissors
- foam brush
- foam glue
- glitter glue
- hot glue gun

- markers
- metal nail
- paintbrush
- pen
- pencil
- poster putty

- ruler
- scissors
- stapler

TIPS

- Before starting a project, read all of the steps and gather all of the supplies needed.
- Work on newspaper or paper towels.
- Ask an adult to help you use a hot glue gun and sharp tools.
- Give glue and paint plenty of time to dry before handling a project.

Star Pencil Topper

This is the cutest craft project! I can't believe it, but it's better than my pink pen. You're going to want to use this precious pony pencil all the time.

You will need:

- adult-sized knit glove
- fabric scissors
- fiber-fill stuffing or cotton balls
- pencil
- rubber band
- thin ribbon
- 2x1-inch (5x2.5 cm) piece of felt
- hot glue
- wiggly eyes
- black permanent marker
- 15 inches (38 cm) fuzzy yarn

optional:
- thin pink ribbon
- rhinestones

1. Cut a finger off the glove, where it joins the hand.

2. Push stuffing into the tip of the finger, filling the finger half full. Put the eraser end of the pencil into the empty part of the finger.

3. Tightly wrap a rubber band around the bottom of the finger and end of the pencil.

4. Tie the ribbon in a double knot, ½ inch (1.3 cm) from the stuffed end of the finger. Push the top of the finger down at an angle. Pull the two ends of the ribbon down and behind the pencil. Tie the ends together in a knot.

5. Cut out two ¾-inch (1.9-cm) felt triangles. Fold each in half and hot glue to the sides of the pony's head (with the openings facing forward). Glue on wiggly eyes. Draw on two nostrils with marker.

6. Cut fuzzy yarn into 3-inch (7.6-cm) pieces. Glue on pieces starting between the ears and down the horse's neck.

Optional: Add a bow to the horse's head and a rhinestone to the reins.

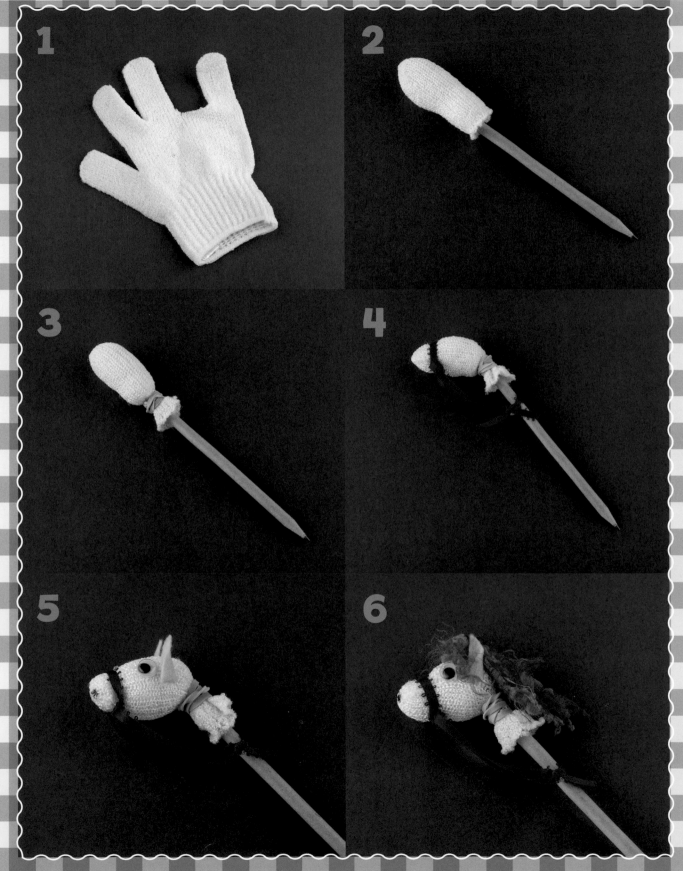

Star Window Decorations

My Granny has stained glass windows, and now I have stained glass stars. I'll make a bunch, so I can pretend I'm beside a campfire looking at the starry sky.

You will need:

- yellow and pink tissue paper
- 6x12-inch (15x30-cm) piece of clear contact paper
- pencil
- paper
- scissors
- marker
- poster putty

optional:
- glitter glue

1. Tear up tissue paper into 1-inch (2.5-cm) pieces.

2. Fold back half of the contact paper backing. Place on a table, sticky side up.

3. Place tissue paper pieces over the sticky contact paper until covered.

4. Slowly press the empty half of the contact paper over the tissue paper. Rub your hand over it to flatten.

5. Draw several star shapes on paper. Cut out. Trace the shapes onto the contact paper with marker. Cut out.

6. Stick a small piece of poster putty to the top point of each star. Press onto a window.

Optional: Decorate stars with glitter glue. Let dry.

Hint:
Tape the corners of the sticky contact paper to a tabletop to make it easier to work with.